Sister Grief:
Defined and Conquered in Jesus

Yvonne Terry-Lewis

WESTBOW
P R E S S®
A DIVISION OF THOMAS NELSON
& ZONDERVAN

WestBow Press books may be ordered through booksellers or by contacting:

WestBow Press
A Division of Thomas Nelson
1663 Liberty Drive
Bloomington, IN 47403
www.westbowpress.com
1-(866) 928-1240

ISBN: 978-1-4908-0657-0 (sc)
ISBN: 978-1-4908-0656-3 (e)

Library of Congress Control Number: 2013915690

Print information available on the last page.

WestBow Press rev. date: 10/28/2019

Table of Contents

Dedication

This book is dedicated in memory of Linda Willis-Burrell, Larry Terry, Michael Terry, Ella Mae Willis, Sheila Pulley, Te'Veria Lee, and Devon Lomax.

Acknowledgments

I thank God for allowing me to feel His love and comfort at the most difficult times in my life. I would like to thank the following people for their support, love, and encouragement during the writing of this book. During my different seasons of grief, these individuals have been a vital part of my Sister Grief and healing. Samuel Willis, my father, Rudolph Lewis, my husband, Antoinette Terry-Brantley and Kiwana Terry, my beautiful daughters, Terino Brantley, my son-in-law, Derek, Troy, Derian, and Shaqunia, my grandchildren, Vincent and Reginald Willis, my brothers, Asandra Willis and Glenda Willis, my loving and devoted sister-in-laws, Bishop Clifford Jonson, my former pastor, Bishop Larry E. Williams, my pastor, and Reginald Price, my good friend, have all played a vital part in my recovery from sister grief. I would be remised if I didn't mention a few other special sister friends, Norma Allen, Jessie Hargrove, Ernestine Holley, Rosa Koonce, and Patsy Tillman. I love each and every one of you as well as other family members and friends who are too numerous to mention. God Bless all of you!

Preface

Grief is universal. All people experience it. It crosses racial lines, social economic classes and religious experiences. Grief comes when we experience loss. We grieve for small losses as well as the big losses. We have all lost something or someone at some time in our lives. I define grief as the way the mind, body, and soul experience and deal with loss. Many people agree that grief is a process that has identifiable stages. These stages are not always identified by the same name, nor are they always linear. Grief counselors and authors writing about grief usually identify between three to six stages. The name given to the various stages in the grief process is not really that important. What is important is that one realizes that certain intense emotions accompany these stages. It doesn't matter how many times you go through the grief process, each loss is different and unique. **Shock** or **denial** is the name I will give to the first stage I experienced. The news of what has happened is a shock to your very being. I experienced some level of shock or denial with the death of each of my loved ones. My most significant occurrences of shock happened after the deaths of my only sister Linda, in 1984, my husband Larry in 1999, my only son, Michael in 2001, my beloved mother, Ella Mae in 2008, my dear friend of over forty years, Te'Veria in 2009 and my 34 year old nephew Devon in 2011. I didn't literally deny that my loved ones had died, but emotionally in my heart I denied that their deaths were real and permanent. I think most people will experience some level of shock when they hear about a loss. They can't believe what they are hearing. In addition to the death of loved ones, we experience grief after a divorce, lost of a job, lost of friendships, and other significant loss. Perhaps one learns that his or her marriage is falling apart. An individual learns that his/her spouse has been having an affair for years. You are devastated! Your company is laying you off after fifteen years on the job. We are often shocked about some of the horrible things we hear or witness through news reports. We are shocked and disturbed by the level of cruelty in the world. As an educator, I have been shocked and amazed by the strength young people exhibit after being exposed to some heart wrenching circumstances. Under circumstances such as these, most people will experience some level of shock or denial.

Another stage is **awareness**. During this stage you come to terms with the reality of what has happened. A sister could possibly experience her worse pain during this stage. It is for real! It will never change. There may be some depression, guilt, fear, anger, doubt, and any other emotion. It is normal to have some level of depression in the awareness stage. Your world has been turned upside down. The key is to determine the length and level of depression. Family and friends can be very helpful during this stage. It is also normal to think about things that may have been done differently. You may question your actions in your mind. Did we go to the doctor in time? Why did I let him get that motorcycle? Did he leave because I gained too much weight? Some sisters experience fear or anger during awareness. How will I make it without him or her? Will I be able to handle things on my own? I can't live without my child. I am so angry. Why did this have to happen to me and my family? I can share with you that I have experienced more than a few of these intense emotions. The length of the awareness stage is different for each sister and each loss. At some point, most people will accept what has happened and begin to rebuild their lives. During acceptance some healing usually begins.

Regardless of the length of the grief process, healthy grief should end with **renewal** or **reconstruction.** I name **reconstruction** as my third stage. When one reaches this point, she has made a conscious decision to put her life together or in some cases begins a totally new life. In this book I will discuss Sister Grief since that is the height, width, and breadth of my experience. The deaths of my sister, husband, son, mother, and friend have so impacted my life that if God had not been in the midst, I would not be alive today to write this book. It is my intent to touch, help, and heal the life of a grieving sister at her point of need.

Introduction

I was compelled to write this book because of the transformation of my life by God after the deaths of my husband of 29 years and my 28-year old son. I began the book about six months after the death of my husband during my reconstruction stage. Writing was therapeutic and healing during my Sister Grief. Life's experiences and grief caused me to stop and start numerous times. After the death of my son Michael, who was killed in a car accident, I had this need to start the book again. I shared my story informally with so many people over the years. I was able to minister to both men and women by listening to their unique and painful stories. God sent me in many different directions spiritually, emotionally, and academically. Spiritually, I moved closer and closer to God as my relationship with Jesus deepened. Emotionally, Jesus helped me to move on as a part of my recovery and reconstruction. In 2002, I enrolled in St. Mary's Seminary to seek a degree in Church Ministries with a concentration in Pastoral Care. Spending more time with God and observing the suffering in this world, caused me to develop deeper compassion and empathy for people in pain. Somehow recognizing the pain of others helped me to heal. My work as a hospice volunteer was interrupted in

May 2004 when I ministered to my mother as she battled cancer. Her fight against the cancer ended on May 23, 2008. After the death of my mother, I knew I had to finish this book. In this book, I plan to share my Sister Grief as well as my experiences with counselors and other grieving sisters. More importantly, I will define Sister Grief and share a plan for conquering grief with Jesus. I pray that other grieving sisters, family members, and friends will be helped by my testimony. God bless!

SISTER GRIEF

Sisters like all people grieve in very individual ways. Some sisters look and act strong by day and cry all night; some cry day and night for a very long time; some turn bitter and push the pain inside; some go around smiling and deny the pain; some run away for awhile until they can deal with the pain; some run away to a sad and desolate place never to return; some indulge in drugs and alcohol; some busy themselves until it's time to fall asleep; some neglect their children and the list of actions and reactions go on and on like an old song. Although God is right there in the midst of the pain waiting to love and hold us and guide us through the grieving process, some will not feel His love or accept His guidance. Some grieving sisters never knew Him; others may know Him and become angry with him because of this horrible loss. Friends, family members, and yes even some churches, do not reach out to these grieving sisters. Sisters, although some of you may not feel it initially, God is there, right where He has always been, loving and wishing the very best for you. You can and will heal with time spent with God and the support of family and friends. Just reach out and touch Jesus; he is always there for you. His telephone line is truly never busy.

MY TESTIMONY

I had a very happy life with a husband, three adult children, three grandsons, mother, father, lots of family and friends, two homes, two cars, and a very good job. The Lord had helped me heal after the death of my only sister in January 1984. His love helped me to rebuild my life in a very meaningful way. But one day, the bottom fell out and my world fell apart. My beloved husband was diagnosed with prostate cancer. Although it was devastating news, we are very strong Christians and we knew everything would be all right. We prayed and fasted and sought the best medical advice. We went through chemotherapy and radiation. My husband would get so tired, but he kept up with the treatment. We all continued to work and pray. I worked at a very demanding job in the Baltimore City Public Schools, yet God allowed me to make every medical appointment and every radiation treatment session. When I think about it now, I ran around like a "mad woman" trying to keep it all together. I know my strength came from the Lord. I went to church and prayed and fasted. This is one sister who knew everything was going to be fine. I had no reason to think otherwise. It had always been that way as far as I could remember. Surely, God would not forsake us. I knew what the doctor said, but this sister was waiting and depending on God to make everything all right. I watched my husband lose weight and refuse to eat. I knew that his inability to do the things that he had been accustomed to deeply concerned him. It was difficult for my children and me to watch him deteriorate. My Larry was a wonderful husband who was very concerned about his family. We were best friends and shared everything.

As soul mates, I felt like this awful pain he was experiencing could be felt down in the depths of my soul. I would call the doctor to get his pain medications increased when he experienced horrible pain. On August 5, 1999, I lost my beloved husband to cancer. The questions I asked myself were: What did I do wrong for God to let my husband die? Did I pray long enough? He was a good man. There are lots of people out there killing people and selling drugs. Lord, why did a good man have to die? In the midst of your storm, you may find yourself asking the same questions. Grief can sometimes cause you to question your faith. This is a normal reaction. Remember how Naomi in the book of Ruth felt after she lost her husband and two sons. She felt as if the Lord himself had turned against her. She told her onlookers to call her "Mara" because she felt God had treated her bitterly. Some of you reading this book may experience some of these same feelings. You may be thinking; why has this terrible thing happened to my family and me? I learned from counseling that some people go into a defense mode. I was one of those persons. I needed to keep busy until I could deal with the pain. I knew that eventually, I had to come to terms with the awful pain I was experiencing. The problem during that time was that to most people everything seemed to be fine. I was able to work and do what I needed to do to get through a day. For a while, all a sister is able to do is get through a day. I experienced problems with sleeping and memory loss. The nights were torturous for me. I often cried myself to sleep. Only God knew my pain. These are normal reactions during Sister Grief. During that time, I just waited and depended on God to make it better. My new favorite scripture became Psalms 27:14. "Wait on the Lord: be of good courage and he shall strengthen thine heart: wait, I say, wait on the Lord."

I had to have hope that things would get better. I knew that Christ's death brought eternal hope for all who believed. Although a Christian woman, I struggled with my deep feelings about loss. There are times in life when the rain pours. I have learned that it really is true that into each life rain will come. I believe that God does not cause the pain, but rather because of the sinful nature of man and because we live in a fallen world, stuff happens.

I did wonder about why so much "stuff" was happening to me. You may be wondering the same thing after much Sister Grief and many sleepless nights, many crying spells, and many days when I felt as if my world was coming to an end. After much grief, one day I could see the light at the end of the tunnel. Every day no longer looked the same. I actually began to look forward to a new day and to time spent with family and friends.

May 2, 2001 did not appear to be different from any other day. On this glorious day the Lord made, I experienced another one of life's storms. My son, Michael, was killed in a car accident. My two daughters and I had the gruesome task of identifying his body. My husband had died two years earlier, and there were no other men available to assist the three of us. Sharing that experience has created a bond among us that can never be broken on this side of glory. We learned from the autopsy that Michael died instantly, however, only our Lord God knew that fact at the time.

My daughter, Kiwana, was the first to receive the news. She of course was devastated, yet the Lord gave her the strength to share this horrific news with me. I know that the Lord was in the midst of her Sister Grief. I thought I was going to lose my mind. I experienced another dose of Sister Grief. I really began to seriously question God. I questioned God over and over again in my mind. "All right now God, I trust you. I know that you love me and didn't send the storms in my life, but where are you now? Why didn't you prevent what happened? I need you now. I can't make it on my own. I was just pulling myself together, but now, here we go again. Family and friends can't always be there.

Will you always be there? I need you Lord! I can't go through this Sister Grief, which I feel way down in the depths of my soul, alone. This lost of my baby boy is unbearable." I have heard from many that losing a child is like no other lost. I literally felt like my whole world had come to an end. As parents we feel we are supposed to protect our children. I asked why my child is dead and I am still alive? My child is supposed to bury me, not I him. If you or a close relative have lost a child, be patient, it will get better. My precious child now dwells in heaven. Oh, how I miss him. I miss him when I see other young men with small children. I miss him at family gatherings when my nephews are around. Actually, I just miss him all the time. The Lord was there for me in my Sister Grief, and he will be there for you in your storm.

After Michael's death, I enrolled at St. Mary's Seminary. I started volunteering with the ill and dying. I had already joined a smaller church to connect better and experience more love and support from the saints. I know now that the move to The Place of Grace Church was orchestrated by God. The love I received after the death of my son was overwhelming. The pastor's wife introduced me to a man who had lost his daughter in a car accident. Another member, whose son had been murdered, became good friends with me. We could share each other's sister grief.

Our friendship and female bond were much like that of Naomi and Ruth in the book of Ruth. Edith Deem (1988), described Ruth as one of the most loving women in the Bible. All the love and support I received after the death of my son helped me to move into the reconstruction stage. During this stage my family and I established a scholarship fund in Michael's name. Awarding scholarships to help young people further their educational endeavors helped our family keep Michael's memory alive. Another way to help yourself is to help others. I found great reward in volunteering at Stella Maris Hospice Center. My volunteering with hospice was interrupted by my mother's diagnosis of Cancer in 2004.

My mother, Ella Mae Willis, died on May 23, 2008. The death of a parent can be devastating. It changes your life in a very special way. As a baby boomer, it was difficult for me to assume the role of parent with my parent. On an intellectual level, we know that our parents will age and die, but on an emotional level we are rarely ready to let go. I will always cherish and miss the special relationship I had with my mother. Mama was a strong woman of God! As the only living female child, I was very devoted to my mother and her care. The time spent caring for my mother was very rewarding and yet demanding. I actually started experiencing Sister Grief before the actual death of my mother. As her condition worsened, I missed her strong motherly advice. Mother was a devout Christian so I was not concerned about her soul, but I missed her great friendship and support. I knew from the past that God would see my family and me through the death of our mother and grandmother. Although the matriarch of our family was no longer living here on earth, we vowed to keep her memory alive. I knew that the love of God would see me through the loss of my mother. In October 2009, as I prepared for my second marriage to Rudolph Lewis, my friend and soul mate, my dear friend TeVeria died suddenly two weeks before my wedding. TeVeria was my dear friend and prayer partner. The shock of her death and deep sense of loss will stay with me for a long time.

Again, God helped me to get through my grief. On August 5, 2011 my family experienced the loss of my nephew. I pray daily for my brother and sister-in-law. This loss was devastating to our family. Grief visited our family once again, but Jesus was there to comfort us all. Now let me share one plan for defining and conquering Sister Grief with Jesus.

CHAPTER 1

S *stands for* SHOCK

Many professionals agree that the first stage of grief is usually shock. Shock is God's way of helping us deal with devastating tragedy such as a loss of a loved one, terminal illness, divorce, horrific accidents and other terrible storms of life. Shock is also part of Sister Grief. Experiencing shock allows a sister to keep it together long enough to do those things that have to be done. For example, in the case of death, many sisters are in shock throughout the whole funeral experience. A sister may not shed tears at this time. She may appear to be so strong even heroic. Friends, family, and clergymen, don't be fooled by this reaction from a grieving sister. She will really need your support in the weeks to come. Sisters tell me that this is also true in the case of divorce and other difficult circumstances. Too often friends, family and even ministers offer a scripture and leave the grieving sister on her own after a few days or weeks. You may feel as if you are all alone. I certainly felt that way for some time. Yet, Jesus is there in the midst of every circumstance and every stage of Sister Grief. However,

Jesus expects believers to be His ambassadors here on earth. He expects those called by His name to exemplify His love.

> "But when the Holy Spirit controls our lives, He will produce this kind of fruit in us: love, joy peace, kindness, goodness, faithfulness . . ."
>
> (Galatians 5:22)

HOW CAN OTHERS HELP DURING THE SHOCK STAGE?

Family members, friends, and church families can be very helpful during this stage. Generally, people take care of the food, make telephone calls, visit and help take care of important details. Instead of offering a lot of advice, this is a time to be a good listener. Let the sister talk if she wants to share. Sharing can be healing for her. Please don't ignore her when she is talking about her loved one or even worse change the subject when she is talking. She may really need to share every detail with you. Be a good listener. This is probably not the best time to quote scripture. Be patient and loving. Let the sister know that God loves her.

MY SHOCK STORY

I experienced the shock stage in the deaths of my loved ones and friends. All admired what they deemed as my strength. I know that the strength that people perceived that I had came from Jesus. Sisters out there experiencing grief, let me share this little secret with you. While in this stage, I was able to eat, sleep, and carry on conversations. I got through the funeral of my sister, husband son, and mother while in this stage. I think it was several weeks before reality set in.

I experienced horrible pain at night and couldn't sleep. I tried reading the Bible, listening to music and watching television. Nothing seemed to work. It was in the midnight hour that this sister called upon the name of the Lord and felt the presence of the Holy Comforter. I called Him night after night for some time.

When my mother died from cancer, I experienced denial at certain times. Usually at the end of the day, I would attempt to call my mother on the telephone before reality set in and I realized that she was really dead. Sisters you will experience shock, the temporary escape from reality. I also experienced shock after the sudden death of my best girl friend Te-Veria. Although we spoke on the telephone everyday, I was not aware of any major illness. We had spoken on the telephone twice the day that she died. I believe I was in shock during her funeral, yet God gave me the strength to keep things together. God sends the Holy Comforter to strengthen us in these most difficult times. Please know that this stage is just that, temporary.

SHOCK—A POEM

> After the death of Larry and Mike I experienced
>   shock to help me cope
> Then one day God removed the block and gave me
>   hope
> He sent me the Holy Comforter to help me deal
>   with the pain,
> After the shock, everything was so real

After loss, life is never the same
You look puzzled and confused
You walk around in a daze
You answer the door and the telephone
All in the midst of your pain
Yes for you, life will never be the same
All of a sudden there is another shock
Mother's illness has run its course
She is no longer here on earth
The entire family misses her life force
So we go through the terrible pain of grief again
Her life impacted Oh so many, children, family,
    friends,
Church members and whosoever will
Nephew gone too soon Wife, children, mother,
    father and sister
Don't despair, the Lord our God does really care,
It will get better
To love is to grieve; Grief is a part of life
And life is a many splendid thing
Sister, know that it does get better
I tell you this in Jesus' name
Peace and blessings for you and me
I love you all and so does He!

CHAPTER 2

I *stands for* INSPIRATION

S isters, at some point after God has begun to help you with the pain; you will need to be inspired. We need a dose or two of inspiration to succeed at most things. Well, so it is with conquering grief. First and foremost, we need to be inspired by the Holy Spirit to get up and face a new day with Jesus. Sometimes it feels better to just lie around and mope. Life does not seem like it is worth living. Pray and ask Jesus to help you get up! We need to be inspired to face all of the changes of life. Know that after loss, life will never be quite the same. Change can be such a difficult beast. We need to be inspired to see ourselves as more than that circumstance. It doesn't matter whether it is the loss of a loved one, the loss of a husband or friend, the lost of a job or any of life's harsh circumstances, we need inspiration. People cannot always be there for you. Jesus is always there. "He delivered us from such a deadly peril, and He will deliver us. On Him we have set our hope that He will deliver us again" II Corinthians 1:10 (ESV). It will take time, but Jesus has all the time in the world. He will wait for you. He loves you!

HOW DO WE GET THIS INSPIRATION?

First, we must reflect on the great love that Jesus has for us. Meditate on His word over and over again. "For God so loved the world that he gave His only begotten Son that whoever believes in him shall not perish but have eternal life" (John 3:16). If we pray to Him and believe with all of our heart that He will be there for us, inspiration will come. This will not happen over night, but after much time spent with Jesus, inspiration will come. You can reach out to others whom you admire to help you get a little inspiration. It starts off simple. You may stay out of bed longer one day. You may look up at the sky with new hope or you may decide to allow a friend to take you for a drive. You are able to focus just a little longer on daily routines. You will suddenly believe that you have a choice. One spiritual counselor, Michael Gerone, who works with March Funeral Home's Grief Support Group in Baltimore says, "you can either choose to adjust or self-destruct." When you get the first bit of inspiration, choose to move forward adjusting to your new life. Go ahead, sister and make your move. You can do it. Jesus is with you!

HOW CAN FAMILY AND FRIENDS HELP?

The role of family and friends during this time is to be available. Make telephone calls and visits. Don't wait for the grieving sister to call you. If you know someone else who has had a similar experience encourage that person to share. Many times the grieving sister does not want to feel that she is worrying others. Invite a grieving sister to a movie or play. Be a good listener!

MY INSPIRATION STORY

I needed inspiration from the Lord to return to work. I really didn't want to return to work after the death of my husband. I prayed and prayed to receive the Lord's guidance. In my case it seemed so much easier to stay at home. I considered retirement. I thought that if I retired everything would be okay. Running away is not usually the best course of action. I learned that retirement was not a realistic option and was not a part of God's plan for me. I was inspired a little each day to move a little closer to return to work. My inspiration came from praying and reading God's word. I was also encouraged by my medical doctor to "get back on the horse". Returning to work brought even more changes in my life. Change had become a dirty word. I was unable to return to my previous position. At a time when my life was turned upside down, I had no choice or input in yet another change. After suffering great pain and loss, I was simply assigned to another school. I called on the Lord to help me move on and persevere at this difficult time. Returning to work three months after Larry's death also meant I would have to face some of the same people, supervisors, who had treated me almost inhumanely at the worst time of my entire life. Although I had worked in the school system for more than twenty-five years, I received little compassion or support from my supervisors at this the worst time in my life. In fact, some seemed to go out of their way to make me suffer. Remember many people put business ahead of any and everything. So many people lack compassion until some tragedy hits their family. One girlfriend who was at her desk crying two weeks after the death of her brother was asked by a co-worker: "Aren't you all over that by now?" My sister friend quickly responded, "when I come to work I have to bring my grief to work with me". It was different after the death of my son. Michael was suddenly killed in an auto accident. The outpouring of love from my family, church, friends, co-workers, strangers and supervisors was phenomenal. The support of the staff, parents and students at my elementary school inspired me to return to work within two weeks. Although I still had a terrible pain, I knew that God would come through for me because He had done it before. Although my church family, biological family, friends, physician and co-workers inspired me to move forward, it was God, our wonderful, gracious, and marvelous Father who gave me the courage and strength to go on. My inspiration came from Jesus and His ambassadors here on earth. One sister friend prayed with me daily. Another sister friend invited me to the movies on almost a weekly basis. One male friend was a good listener and spoke with me often. Again, I tell you Jesus will do the same for you, if you let Him. It's not easy. Another time when I sought inspiration from the Lord was when I retired in 2007 to care for my terminally ill mother. Rather than risk rebuff and or a lack of empathy from supervisors as I attended to the needs of my mother, the Lord guided me towards retirement. After thirty-four years with the Baltimore School System, I retired at the age of fifty-six. The decision to retire was the best decision that I could have made.

I was able to spend quality time with my mother as she transitioned to her new life. After her death, I was inspired to honor her memory by helping my father and other family members. With God all things are possible. You may feel like no one understands. Some will understand and others will not. Please know that you can do it. Make your move today. Take that first step!

INSPIRATION-A POEM

Death of a loved one can causes so much pain
For you life will never be the same
At that terrible point of desperation
Peeking through the clouds comes Inspiration
Where does it come from?
Inspiration, Inspiration, Inspiration
I got out of bed early today
I went to the movies today
I talked to the insurance agent
I even returned several telephone calls
Our Father in heaven sends us peace and blessings
He is the only one who can stop the rain
Thank you oh Lord for easing the pain
We are inspired to go on and live life again
We can go on and survive because He is our friend
He gives us inspiration to live
To live life more abundantly
Thank you God for your Inspiration!

CHAPTER 3

S *stands for* SHARING

S haring your feelings with family and friends is so important. It is an important strategy that will help you conquer your Sister Grief. Although many times family and friends want to protect you by not talking about your loss, talking and sharing is exactly what you need to do to heal. Find one special friend who is willing to listen and allow you to share your deepest thoughts. In my case, there were two special friends who listened to me constantly. One served as a prayer partner and listening buddy. The other received so many letters from me which conveyed my deepest feelings. I will always remember the support of Teveria, my now deceased friend and Reggie my good spiritual friend. Both of these friends along with so many other family members and friends were instrumental to my healing after the death of my husband and son. God sent others my way to lend support after the death of my mother.

How Can Family and Friends Help With The Sharing?

If you have a church family, it can help with the sharing. Church members can reach out to a grieving sister. They can make telephone calls and come by to visit the sister. Pastors can get sisters in touch with other sisters who have had similar losses. Don't be surprised if your church family does not share with you much after the funeral. Many churches feel their responsibility ends after the funeral. If you don't get a call from members of your church family or receive a visit, don't allow this to cloud your view of God. What is your God-Image? My God-Image is one of a loving Father. Yes, bad things happen but God does not cause these things to happen. Man has free will and sometimes things just happen. People are human and sometimes don't know what to say. In addition, we live in a hurried society. Everyone is so busy living their lives. Remember any failure is not in God, but in imperfect humans. Please don't allow well-meaning Christians to make you feel guilty about grieving. Grieving is a normal process. The need to share and release feelings is necessary and a part of Sister Grief. Family and friends can serve as excellent listeners; it will mean so much to a sister. You can share personal experiences of others if it is appropriate. The most important thing to share with a grieving sister is your love for her. I encourage every grieving sister to allow family and friends to share her pain in love.

FORMAL SHARING SESSIONS

There are times when sharing in a formal group setting can be very helpful. I strongly recommend support groups and grief-counseling sessions. I have participated in both individual and group counseling sessions. Many states have Compassionate Friends, a support group for bereaved parents. There are groups for widows and widowers, and children. Many hospice organizations sponsor support groups. Grief is a normal process, but there are times when one may need additional support from well trained professionals. Please don't allow anyone to make you feel guilty for seeking help. I have met so many people who shared that their participation in a support group changed their lives. I found the support groups that I participated in to be invaluable to my healing.

HOLIDAYS AND OTHER SPECIAL DAYS

On holidays and anniversaries, it may be difficult to share. Your loss may seem so painful that all you want to do is run away and hide. One sister shared she took off from work on every anniversary of her mother's death. She said she just needed to be alone on that day. While life has changed for you, in most cases it is best to be with people who care about you. You may want to plan ahead of time for holidays and other special days. The day is on the calendar and will come. I knew that holidays were going to be difficult for me so I planned with my family ahead of time. I anticipated that there would be sadness, but at the same time I focused on what was good. The first round of holidays and anniversaries were the worse for me and my family. On the anniversaries of the deaths, we held special memorial services at family dinners. At Thanksgiving and Christmas we recalled fond or special memories about our loved ones. Regardless of what you decide to do, anticipate that there may be more sadness than on other days. Please feel free to cry as often as you need too. Anticipate that the anniversary of the death of your loved one may cause discomfort. The first Mother's Day after the death of your mother will be sad. This is normal! After a divorce, your wedding anniversary date can bring back both good and bad memories. Although we cannot stop holidays and anniversaries from coming, we can share our feelings with our loved ones. There needs to be a time of sharing.

SHARING—A POEM

> Allow your family and friends to show that they care
> Reach out to them and share your feelings
> They will embrace you and help with the healing
> The Lord is there in the midst of your pain
> He will send the Holy Comforter who can
> > stop the rain
> The rain poured and poured while you grieved
> But the Lord will heal if you only believe
> Once you believe, you can share and care
> For other grieving souls who might not be there
> Sharing and caring is a part of God's Plan
> Agape love is what He wants for this land, Earth

CHAPTER 4

T *stands for* TRUST

"You will keep in perfect peace him whose mind is steadfast, because he trusts you" (Isaiah 26:3). Sisters, as you begin to trust that God loves you, you will move through the grieving process realizing healing and peace. You will begin to trust that you can adjust in a productive way to a new life. You will begin to trust other people again. You will begin to trust that you have the power to make it. You will trust that the Lord will supply all of your needs. Read and trust his word. The Lord will send the special people who will be your support in those difficult moments. You must allow yourself to trust family and friends. The most important thing to realize is that you can trust God to do what is best for you. God loves you!

HOW CAN I LEARN TO TRUST?

Pray, Pray, Pray, about trusting people. Above all trust that the Lord loves you. "Blessed is the man who trusts in the

Lord, whose confidence is in Him. He will be like a tree planted by the water that sends out its roots by the stream. It does not fear when heat comes: its leaves are always green. It has no worries in a year of drought and never fails to bear fruit" (Jeremiah 17:7-8).A sister can start to trust by allowing the people you already trust to help you. Family and friends are the easiest people for us to trust. If you have been hurt by family or friends, pray to the Lord for guidance. You will need to forgive! Allow the Holy Spirit to show you how to forgive. Observe people to learn who you can trust. People who keep their commitments and who are good listeners can usually be trusted in difficult times. Sisters, there may be a pastor, counselor, or church member who exhibits the fruit of the spirit. Watch for those individuals who seem to have the gift of compassion and who have proved themselves to be trustworthy. It is sad to say, but not all Christians are trustworthy. The Lord will lead and guide you, but you must open your heart and listen. He will send that special person who will be there for you. Be open. You may feel as if you have no one. I would like to suggest that there is usually at least one person that God will send your way. Accept the help and support that this person offers you. Your ambassador from God may just be there to listen to you at a very difficult and sad moment. Perhaps you and your trusted friend can share a movie together. If the person who died was your husband, significant other, or a male relative such as a father or brother, you may find it difficult to trust another male.

The pain you feel is so great that you do not want to take a chance on experiencing anything like that again. You also understand that your loved one can not be replaced, of course that is exactly right! You don't want to replace anyone, but you do want to live again in a new way. Take your time and seek counsel from the Lord in this regard. Allowing yourself to develop a friendship with a male can be a very positive thing. God intended for us sisters to complement the man. So as difficult as it may be, we must learn to trust ourselves and the positive males who will come along to support us in our healing. We have to trust God and wait on Him.

HOW CAN FAMILY AND FRIENDS HELP?

The most important thing you can do to help a grieving sister with trust is to be trustworthy. Don't make promises that you do not intend to keep. Sister Grief can make a sister very sensitive. You may not think much of a broken promise, but to the grieving sister it reinforces her feelings of abandonment. Family and friends make a special effort to be loving and trustworthy during Sister Grief. Keep your promises to a grieving sister; it is very important for the sister to experience your trustworthiness.

MY TRUST STORY

I am an independent person, so it was difficult for me to ask others for help and then trust them to come through for me. This was something I had to learn to do. My husband, son, and mother were always there for me and my daughters. My husband and I were so close. We did everything together.

Everyone who knew us saw us as inseparable. After the death of my husband Larry, my son took over as the man of the house. He was very protective of my daughters and me. Although he grieved the death of his father, he felt it was his responsibility to look out for the females in the family. His own personal grief was unresolved because he tried to take care of everyone On May 2, 2001, I experienced the terrible pain of my son's death. I didn't have a great deal of trust in life at the time. During the shock stage and even the awareness stage, I didn't trust that I could make it to the next day. You may feel the same way. Our marvelous God came to me night after night like a great lover reassuring me that I could trust Him. He reminded me of the great love that he had for me. He let me know that I could completely depend on Him. He helped me to learn to trust others, especially males. Unfortunately very few males have experience supporting sisters during grief. Many have been reared to exhibit a tough rigid attitude. In the process of learning to trust others, I learned to accept and understand that people are busy and can not always keep their promises. My whole world was turned upside down, yet the sun still rose every morning. Life and living continued as usual for all those around me. I had to reach up and grasp it or be swallowed whole by this terrible sister grief. I had to learn to trust, regardless of how bad I felt at the time. Please trust that the Lord will send the right people along at the right time. Trust that these people are a part of your life for a reason or a season. As with love, when you trust people, there may be a few who let you down. I experienced the deep pain of being rejected by two sister friends. One betrayed me in a financial matter and the other made very insensitive comments. I have learned that although you may lose friends during the storms of life, our friend Jesus will be with us always. God in his infinite wisdom will send the right people along to support you. You have to trust and open up your heart. During each of my losses, God sent special people to be a part of my healing.

After the death of my only sister, Linda, many special sisters came into my life. After the deaths of my husband and son, some friendships reached new levels while other friendships were developed. At the time of my mother's death in 2008, God placed several older women of grace in my life. These strong women of God helped me heal during this sad time. While no one could take my mother's place, they did help to fill a void in my life. God will send ambassadors to you during your time of need. We must love and trust one another. Sometimes this is difficult, but we know that everything is possible with our Lord. You can do it!

TRUST A POEM

In the midst of the pain it is so hard to trust
But know that our Lord above has a plan for all of us
Sister, the pain that you suffered was oh so great
But the Lord above will help you handle everything
    on your plate
Others will come along to help you heal
Accept their help until you again learn to feel
Accept the love of a Holy God and all His
    ambassadors

For they will help you accept all His love and more
So look to the future and that very bright light
Trust and obey Him and you will win this fight
Trust, Trust, Trust the Lord above
He has so much to give you especially His love
He so loved us all He gave His only begotten son to
    die on a cross for us!
Amen

CHAPTER 5

E *stands for*
ENCOURAGEMENT

Sisters who have suffered grief truly need encouragement. Even those who have a strong relationship with God need encouragement. We are all human and can feel discouraged when we reach a low point. We need to know or be reminded that regardless of how bad it is now, it will and can get better. When you are in the midst of the pain and sorrow, it is difficult to believe that it will ever get better. You feel as if you are all alone. First, let me share with you that God is there and will never leave you. He will send His disciples here on earth to help encourage us in the most difficult times. Although it may not feel like it right now, his plans for us are good. "For I know the plans I have for you," declares the Lord, "plans to prosper you and not to harm you, plans to give you hope and a future" (Jeremiah 29:11).

HOW CAN I ENCOURAGE MYSELF?

Sometimes we have to do things to encourage ourselves. Keeping a record of your experiences in a journal and documenting your successes is a good way to encourage yourself. When I read my early journal entries and compared them to my later entries my growth in the grieving process was evident. My early entries were sad and full of despair. Reward yourself for the small steps that you take toward moving on. Buy yourself a new dress or new pair of shoes. Encourage yourself with the Word of God. Stay in the Word. The sword of the Spirit, which is the Word of God, can be both an offensive and defensive weapon. The Word is whatever we need it to be at the time. The Word is powerful and will be healing to your very soul. After being encouraged by the Word, you are more able to encourage yourself. Focus on a favorite scripture or a favorite song to get you through. I listened to many of Yolanda Adams' songs to encourage myself. Listen to your favorite inspirational artists.

HOW CAN FAMILY AND FRIENDS HELP?

The responsibility of family and friends is to encourage a grieving or struggling sister. The sisterhood can serve as a strong support system for someone who is going through a traumatic experience. This is not a time for envy or strife. Lift a sister up! The role of the family and friends is to support sisters who have lost a loved one, gone through a divorce and or suffered abuse. When a sister is struggling with a wayward child, family and friends should be there for her. Sometimes encouragement involves getting a sister involved in a productive job or project. Friends can encourage a sister by sharing the promises of God in the Word of God. Encouragement is helping someone hold on to his or her faith. In some instances you may need to encourage a sister to reconnect with her faith or even to accept the love of Jesus for the first time. Be a good ambassador for Christ and extend His love to a grieving sister.

MY ENCOURAGEMENT STORY

As previously mentioned, I have experienced the death of many close family members and friends. After each death, the Lord almighty sent special people into my life to encourage me. Sometimes encouragement came from longtime friends such as sister friends who prayed with me. The girls prayed with and for me during my most painful experiences. After the deaths of my husband and son, my mother and sister-in-law were always there to share an encouraging word at the right time. Thank God for devoted mothers. The sisters in my women's club and book club were also very supportive. During that period my pastors, David and Althea Franklin were a great source of comfort to my family and me. My brothers volunteered to help around the house from time to time, which proved to be a great source of encouragement. I also benefitted greatly from the encouragement I received from support groups such as, A TIME OF SHARING, sponsored by March Funeral Home, and my individual grief counseling sponsored by Stella Maris. Grief is universal and will visit us over and over again. After the death of my mother in 2008, I received encouragement from family, friends, co-workers and my church family. One special friend, Ernestine, took the lead role of supporter during my mother's illness. Our entire family received encouragement and support during her four year battle with Cancer. It was very encouraging to my family to feel the love of so many people as they ministered to mother. People came by to pray, sing songs, and read. It was truly a blessing from God. The sisterhood was strong when my dear friend and prayer partner died at the age of 57. The other sister friends and I bonded closer together and supported each other. We encouraged each other day by day as we learned to accept that our group would no longer be the same. It made us appreciate those of us that are left even more. At every turn, there were ambassadors sent from God to encourage me in each storm. He did it for me and He will do it for you

ENCOURAGEMENT—A POEM

While I drowned myself in despair
It seemed as if no one even cared
But the Lord who loves me best
Would not let me fail this test
He sent so many who were so dear
To encourage me not to have fear
They telephoned, sent flowers and came by
Some just came, listened and watched me cry
They encouraged me to have faith and hold his hand
Because God is in control of the Master Plan

CHAPTER 6

R *stands for* RECONCILIATION

After a death or crisis we may feel that God has abandoned us. It is normal after a tragedy to question God. Often your faith is shaken because you are in so much pain. Well meaning Christians will try to make you feel guilty about your feelings. Your grief is personal to you. You must work through it. Reconciliation is recognizing that without Christ we are apart from God and can accomplish nothing. "I am the vine, you are the branches, if a man remains in me and I remain in Him, he will bear much fruit, apart from me you can do nothing" (John 15:5). Reconciliation comes through faith and brings peace. Sometimes there are family members and friends that you need to forgive so that you are able to move on. The pain of what happened is often real. You feel raw, angry or just hurt. Pray to God to help you to forgive. If you stay there in bitterness with an unforgiving spirit, it will hurt you more than them. It will also delay if not prevent your recovery. As difficult as it may be, write that letter, make that telephone call, and take that first big step.

HOW CAN I FORGIVE THOSE WHO HURT ME?

First reflect on God's great love for us. Visualize Christ dying on the cross for our sins. Think about the goodness of God daily. Read scriptures and pray daily. Think about a time when someone had to forgive you. Although your hurt has come at this awful time, remember your pain is personal to you. Others may have empathy or sympathy, but no one feels quite like you. Forgive so that you can move on to a better time. It is difficult, but you can do it. Do it today.

WHAT CAN FAMILY AND FRIENDS DO TO HELP WITH RECONCILIATION?

As family and friends, your role is to pray and listen. Understand that much of what a sister feels is based on her emotional state. In some cases the anger and hurt she feels towards someone is justified. Whether justified or not, the grieving sisters need reconciliation to occur so that she is able to heal. When the sister's anger is directed at a hospital or doctor, you should listen and gently say to her that the doctor did all that he could. When she is angry at a family member, regardless of whether it is justified or not justified, you might say, "I hear what you are saying, I know you are hurting now. Give it some time before you make a final decision. I am here if you need me." Basically, it is the sister who must come to grips with forgiveness. As she continues to focus on the Lord, things usually get better. It is probably not a good idea to quote scripture unless she requests that you do so. Just be a friend and a good listener.

MY RECONCILIATION STORY

In my own experience reconciliation was vital. There were so many who unintentionally caused pain at very difficult times in my life. Although some people deliberately did hurtful things, most of the hurt was unintentional. I had to learn to forgive to move forward. I had to forgive the large church family and busy pastor who did not take the time to call me after my husband's death. I now know that his actions were not intended to hurt me. But they did hurt at the time. People are human, and therefore can not always be there for you. People are busy and have other priorities, but our God is never too busy for any of us. I had to forgive this one supervisor who treated me almost inhumanly during one of the worst years in my life. This person appeared to be void of empathy or sympathy. Sometimes it appeared as if this person went out of his way to be cruel. I had to forgive some family members and friends who were insensitive after the deaths of my husband and son. I had to forget a few friends who said unkind words during this difficult time. I have learned that people often just do not know what to say, so they say things that are sometimes insensitive. My understanding and forgiveness did not happen right away, but it did happen. I can honestly tell you that with Jesus I am a better person because of my ability to forgive. It will take time but nothing is too difficult for God. You can forgive because of Jesus. He will help you forgive. Move towards forgiveness now!

RECONCILIATION—A POEM

I will take that first step to forgive
It's really the only way to live
Jesus died for the sins of you and me
I must try to be as forgiving as He
Let's love one another with all our heart
After a pain so great it hurt my whole heart
Reconciliation helps towards making a new start
It's what I had to do
You have to do it too
God loves you!

CHAPTER 7

G *stands for* GRACE

Your pain is so great that you question if you were under the Grace of God? You think to yourself, where is Grace now? Although we do not deserve it, God has given us His kindness and mercy and has saved us for His glory. Jesus died on the cross for you my sister. Although you don't feel it at this moment, you will find that His grace really is sufficient. You may have lost your husband, your son, your daughter, your mother, your father, your grandmother, or some other beloved family member or friend. You feel hopeless. You didn't feel any grace. Where is mercy? You may be thinking, Lord, my husband left me with six children. Lord, the job fired me after working there fifteen years. Does this sound familiar? Grace begins with God and is given freely. It is His unmerited favor in our lives even when we are going through. So even when we are hurting, let us go boldly to the throne of our gracious God. There we will receive mercy and power to go on. "Let us then approach the throne of grace with confidence, so that we may receive mercy and find grace to help us in our time of need" (Hebrews 4:16). It will take some time, but you will eventually recognize the grace of God after your long struggle. God is always there in the midst of our storms.

HOW CAN I FEEL HIS GRACE?

There are some actions that we must take to feel that loving Grace after a crisis or tragedy. We must act! First, we must pray without ceasing. We must have an attitude of prayer. Get a trusted friend to be your prayer partner. My good friend TeVeria, who is with God now, served as my special prayer partner. We are at a low point and Satan would desire to take control of our minds. We can not allow that to happen. Your prayer partner can encourage you and stand in the gap when you are down. In the last week of my prayer partner's life I did all the praying. I did not know at that time that God had me to stand in the gap for my dear friend. As I reflect on this now, it is a source of comfort. In addition to my main prayer partner, my sister-in-law Asandra and my friend Reggie prayed with me on occasion. I know that they played a vital part in my healing process. Next, read the word daily and wait on the Lord. Praise Him while you are waiting for your break through. In time you really will feel better. Practice being in His presence at home and in fellowship with other believers. Let God show His Grace through others. Get out and attend some social functions even if you don't feel like it. Write your thoughts in a journal. Listen to gospel music or music that soothes so that you will feel His peace or Grace on a daily basis. Cry when you feel like crying. It's good for you. His Grace really is sufficient. Read books about healing and spend time with the saints who exhibit the fruit of encouragement and love. "The Lord is merciful and gracious; he is slow to anger and full of unfailing love" (Psalms 103:8).

MY GRACE STORY

I prayed without ceasing. When my prayer partner was not available, I prayed with other saints that I trusted. I prayed late into the evenings. All of this praying was going on even while I maintained the appearance of full recovery. It was only an appearance, but I knew it would get better because of the trust I had in God and His Grace. I read scripture daily. I focused on those scriptures that emphasized Jesus' great love for me. After the death of my husband, my new church, The Place of Grace, was just that, a place where I felt the Grace and love of God. I forced myself to get out and stay active. I enlisted the aide of a few trusted friends in this endeavor. Rosa, a dear friend, and I went to the movies on a regular basis. I continued to write in my journal and read numerous books dealing with grief, healing and moving on. I thank God for the many friends and family who were there to help with the healing. Just as I began to heal, my son Michael died in a traffic accident. I thought I would also die and felt no Grace from God. Although I didn't understand anything that had happened, I trusted God. I continued to pray, fast, and meditate. God told me to get up from my bed of affliction and help someone else. In 2002, I started matriculating at St. Mary's Seminary in Baltimore, Maryland. I found my study to be another way to get closer to God. I became friends with the only African American librarian at St. Mary's Seminary. After a seven year friendship, Rudolph Lewis would become my second husband in 2009. It was in 2002 that I also started volunteering at Mercy Hospital and Stella Maris Hospice Center. When we hurt, it helps if we can reach out and help someone else. When you take your eyes off your situation, you realize that you are not alone in suffering. My volunteering was an amazing experience that helped me in my healing. It was also in 2002 that some of my family and friends helped me to start the Michael D. Terry Scholarship Fund. The board has given several college scholarships each year since its inception. I experienced the death of my precious mother in 2008. Although this was a very painful experience, I knew that eventually things would get better and I would experience God's miraculous Grace once again. Although each death has touched me in a painful and very unique way, one constant has been the Grace of God. The Grace of God can truly heal our mind, body, and soul. Hallelujah!

GRACE—A POEM

The Lord is full of Amazing Grace
In times of sorrow He helps us find our place
Although I have experienced terrible pain
And life for me will never be the same
As I look to Him to get through each day
His love and tender mercies show me the way
So on this daily journey I seek His face
Because He truly is full of Amazing Grace
His Grace is sufficient!

CHAPTER 8

R *stands for* RESOLUTION

R esolution in the context of Sister Grief refers to a sister reaching that point when a decision is made to make a change and look to the future. Resolution is about choice. Sisters can resolve to reorganize their lives or become disorganized and disenchanted in the grief. Remember we said we grieve all sorts of losses. It could be a case of divorce, loss of a job, or the death of a loved one. Please know that it will take time to work through the process, but resolution must occur at some point. Most of us will experience at some time or another all the emotions associated with grief such as fear, anger, jealousy, or love. These are natural emotions. Why is my son dead and not hers? We are in danger of becoming ill if we experience distorted emotions such as anxiety, bitterness, helplessness, ugly envy, low self-esteem, depression, or self-pity for a prolonged period of time. Some unresolved issues in our lives may cause us to experience these distorted emotions. At some point during the grief process for resolution to occur, we must look to the future and recognize our lives have changed. I use the term reorganize here because it is true that after a loss life will never be exactly the same. This is true in the case of the death of a loved one, but it is also true in the case of divorce, lost of a job, lost of a deep friendship or in the case of any tragic event.

WHAT CAN YOU DO TO REACH RESOLUTION?

I have said that to be healthy resolution must occur, but I suppose you are wondering how a sister is supposed to make the change. My inspiration comes from the Word of God. I call your attention to two strong women in the Bible. Ruth and Esther stand out as brave women who survived the most difficult of circumstances to learn God's plans for their lives. The Word of God tells us that Jesus will never leave or forsake us. Just like women in the Bible, many women who are right in our midst overcome great circumstances everyday. Often when women face trials, they allow God to transform their pain into a powerful source in Kingdom building. Terrible grief and pain helped to produce MADD—Mothers Against Drunk Driving. After the death of my son, my family and I started the Michael D. Terry Scholarship Board to award scholarships to students in support of their post-secondary education. We can make a choice to go on in the midst of difficult situations because we know we are not alone. He is with us! Sister, this very day choose to look to the future. I know that it may be a strange and uncertain future, but our Lord knows our destiny. Use all of the strategies that have been discussed previously and resolve that this is the day that you look towards the future regardless of how different and difficult that will be after your loss. There will be some setbacks along the way, but that is okay because the Lord will be there to pick you right back up. You can do it. Take it one day at a time.

MY RESOLUTION STORY

After each significant loss in my life, there had to be resolution. My only sister died in 1984. We were very close and spent a lot of time together. It was after the death of my sister that I decided to continue my education and began to work on my master's degree. After some time, there was peace, hope, and finally resolution. In 1999, after the death of my husband, I realized that my life would never be the same. My partner, lover, supporter, and best friend was gone forever. During the grieving process, which was very difficult, I had to learn to adjust to life without Larry in it. I was no longer a wife, lover or friend to Larry. I had to make some major adjustments. I know that some of you will have to do the same. Making the necessary adjustments was hard work that was tragically interrupted and changed after the death of my son. His death was a sudden loss that left me totally unprepared as if one could ever really prepare for the loss of a child. The adjustment of living in this world with one of my children missing is one that I am still struggling with, but I tell you I had to learn to adjust. I believe that if I had not chosen to allow Jesus to help me make a choice to live a new life; I believe that I would have died. I feel that pieces of me died with the deaths of my sister, husband and son. Even after these significant losses in my life, I experienced more loss. My dear mother died in 2008, and my best girlfriend died suddenly in 2009. After each loss, I experienced all the stages of sister grief. After the deaths of my husband and son, I needed the love of God like never before in my life. At this stage in my life, I have resolved to allow Jesus to guide my every step. I will listen to His voice and do those things which are pleasing in His sight. Yes, I know that sometimes I will fail, but I also know that God's Grace is sufficient. If we fail while we are going through the grief process, He will pick us up. Although I have resolved to go on and live, I tell you that I still have difficult days from time to time. Anniversaries and holidays are still difficult, but I prepare for them by planning ahead. As sisters, we are expected to keep the family together. When we hurt, the Lord will be there to nurture us. Let Him hold you in His loving arms. Resolve to live!

RESOLUTION A—POEM

In the midst of Sister Grief there is resolution
Be certain that God is a part of the solution
This terrible pain must leave; it calls for choice
Look to God in times like these to design the next
    course
He designed the master plan that covers all life
Your life was not designed to be filled with strife
Jeremiah twenty-nine eleven says "I know the plans I
    have for you
So look to Him at this time of great need
For Him supplying the love and peace you need is not
    a great deed

This is the love and peace that surpasses all
    understanding in this world
Feeling that special love of God makes you a very
    special sister girl!

CHAPTER 9

I *stands for* INTIMACY

HOW CAN I BECOME INTIMATE AGAIN?

It will be difficult to become truly intimate again once you have been hurt and experienced Sister Grief. This deep pain could come from a broken heart due to an unfaithful husband or significant other. It could come from a divorce after 10 or 15 years of devotion to a husband and the marriage. It could even come from hurt of a broken sister-to-sister relationship based on betrayal. In my case, my deep pain comes from the deaths of loved ones and friends. Their lives seemed to end much too soon. The pain is so great that you wonder if you will share that kind of intimacy again or if you even want to. I have learned to receive pure love. You must develop or deepen the intimacy you have with Jesus Christ. His kind of love never hurts; it's everlasting, comforting, strengthening and full of pure power. His intimacy gives you strength to go on and become a true survivor (Psalms 103: 20). For His unfailing love is as great as the height of the heavens above the earth . . .

(Hosea 2:16-20) "In that coming day," says the Lord, "you will be my husband, instead of my master . . . I will make you my wife forever, showing your righteousness and justice, unfailing love to you and make you mine, and you will finally know me as Lord." "The Lord is with us always. Reach out and feel His love. Walk and talk with Him daily. My brother, Pastor Reginald Willis says, "we must receive God's intimate counsel. God is both our counselor and comforter". Once you have developed or deepened your relationship with Jesus you will be able to reach out to others and love again. Although it may seem difficult, start small with extending kindness and friendship to others in need. Call on friends that you feel you can trust. Once you are able to love yourself again the way God loves you, others will be attracted to you. Your light will shine brightly. Understand that since only God's love is 100% pure, there is some risk involved in trusting and loving again. You may get hurt, but here is where the old cliché, "it is better to have loved and lost, than never to have loved at all" seems to apply. God is love and He created us to love.

MY INTIMACY STORY

I know to love and trust again is risky. There is always the possibility that you may experience pain again. I know this experience first hand. After the death of my husband, the one man that I trusted and reached out to, did not seem to share my feelings. I can admit now that I didn't know about dating or the way today's single men think. I had been in a long lasting marriage for 29 years. I learned more about men and how they think and feel by reading and talking to male friends. I have always been a good listener and conversationalist. I missed the friendship that I enjoyed with my husband. I believe I tried too hard to make my first relationship with a male after the death of my husband a duplication of my marriage. It may have been too much for my friend, a life-long bachelor. We were at different places. I have since learned that he was attracted to the Jesus in me, we did really love each other, but only as Jesus loves. I had to learn that things had changed and life would never be exactly the same. I had to take the time to get to know myself better and deepen my relationship with Jesus, the lover of my soul. I learned to embrace my new life and be happy with myself and my family and friends. I met my new husband, Rudy, three years after the death of my husband.

We shared a love of God, African and African-American history and culture, reading, writing, and music. After a seven year friendship, which had its ups and downs, we married in 2009. Many family and friends shared in our celebration of love. I believe God has a plan for each of us. Sisters, each of us have a unique plan designed by God. Some may marry, but marriage is not in the plan for every sister. Trust the Lord God with all your heart and soul. Let Him love you like no other can love you. God will truly supply all your needs. WAIT ON HIM!

INTIMACY—A POEM

The love of God is the greatest love of all
He loves even when we stumble and fall
He is always there to answer our call
There are times when we experience deep, deep pain

Times when we know life will never be the same
His love and comfort is there in the midst of it all
He handles all circumstances the great and the small
Lord, oh Lord thank you for hearing me when I pray
I know because of your love that the pain will
　　　one day go away
I love you for the intimacy we have and your caring way!

CHAPTER 10

E *stands for* EXAMPLE

When you are experiencing Sister Grief you need positive role models or examples. You need to talk and fellowship with others who are survivors of grief. If your husband has left you, fellowship with a sister who has overcome that betrayal. If you are grieving because your son and/or daughter is in jail; join a support group and fellowship with other parents who are experiencing or have experienced the same thing. If you are divorced, fellowship with other divorcees who are living a positive life. If you experience a great loss due to death, fellowship with other bereaved sisters and or families. Join a support group for survivors of grief. You may also look for examples in the Bible. The Bible is a great source of inspiration and has all the role models we need. Reflect again on the story of Ruth and Naomi in the book of Ruth. Naomi lost her husband and both of her sons in a foreign land. She felt that the Lord had turned against her. Initially, Naomi was a bitter woman, but Naomi overcame bitterness and was able to feel the love of God once more. Ruth loss her husband, but vowed to live by her mother-in-law's side forever. As a young widow who is devoted to her mother-in-law, Ruth finds love again in Boaz. We must look around us and find modern examples of Ruth, Naomi, The Virgin Mary, Mary Magdalene, Esther, Deborah, and many others.

HOW CAN I FIND POSITIVE EXAMPLES OF SURVIVORS?

God is our best example of love and goodness. He is our ultimate example. Jesus on the cross is the best example of unconditional love. He provides ambassadors here on earth to implement His plan. Look for positive examples of people who exhibit God's love in your everyday life. You can find people who exhibit admirable character on your job, in church, in support groups, in schools, in a store, or anywhere that you happen to be. Seek support from your church family if possible. Find a prayer partner with whom you can share your deepest thoughts. Seek out those positive examples that God has placed in your midst to help you at this crucial time. "Just as the suffering of Christ flows over into our lives, so also through Christ our comfort overflows" (II Corinthians 1:5).

MY EXAMPLE STORY

I received invaluable support from both individual counseling as well as group counseling. The conversations I had with others who had loss an adult child were invaluable to me. One man who had loss his daughter in a traffic accident talked with me on a regular basis. I also spoke and dined regularly with a woman from my church whose adult son had been murdered. We were a support to each other. She served as an example of a sister who experienced a loss similar to my own. I found the newsletters and support offered by Compassionate Friends to be helpful. As I mentioned earlier, look for examples of survivors in the Bible. There are a myriad of self health books available. Secondly, you can serve as an example of a survivor with the Lord's help. I know that my faith in the Lord gave me the strength to go on and to even write this book. Friends and family applauded me for my strength. I thank the Lord for the strength they saw in me. It was the Lord who made me a woman of strength. Look to the Lord from whence comes your help. The ultimate role model for us all is Jesus (I Corinthians 11:1).

"And you should follow my example, just as I follow Christ's" (Matthew 5:13). You are the salt of the earth. But what good is salt if it has lost its flavor? Sister, you are the salt of the earth. Don't let this grief allow you to permanently lose your flavor. I can tell you from personal experience that Joy does come in the morning. Don't feel bad if the morning takes a while to arrive. It will come!

EXAMPLE—A POEM

Look to the Lord as the great example
His love is everlasting through trials and tribulations
Though in this life pain and suffering we all must
    sample

Faith in His wondrous healing power brings about
    restoration
He will strengthen you and give you all power in
    your hands
But then you must become a 21st century disciple,
and share the good news all over the land
People are hurting and need to learn of His plan
They need to know about the blood that was shared
because of His great love for mankind
God loves us and will never leave us alone
The Holy Comforter was left with us to love, comfort,
    and lead Us
to His great Agape Love
Pray, pray and pray
Let the grace of the Lord be with you always!

CHAPTER 11

F *stands for* FAITH *and* FRIENDSHIP

F aith is the confident assurance that we will always receive what we hope for if it is in the will of God. During difficult times while we are experiencing Sister Grief we hope most of all that this awful pain will go away. Regardless of how we may be feeling at the time, having faith in the promises of God can help to sustain us. There are countless examples of biblical characters who exhibited great faith. Our faith will be strengthened when we read about Abraham and Sarah of the Old Testament. There are so many sisters who have experienced tragedies, but who now have full lives. These sisters not only serve as examples of people who have persevered, but we can look to them to strengthen our faith. Your storm seems as if it will never end, but the Lord God assures us that it will. Wait on Him. So sisters when everything seems to be falling apart and there does not appear to be any hope. Hold on to your faith. "Faith is being sure of what we hope for and certain of what we do not see" (Hebrews 11:1).

HOW CAN I HOLD ON TO MY FAITH?

Attend worship at a Bible teaching and believing church. Faith comes by hearing. Read about people who had great faith in the Bible. In addition to Abraham, a man of great faith, there are numerous examples of men and women in the Bible who exercised great faith. The woman with an issue of blood demonstrated great faith because she believed that if she could just touch the hem of His garment she would be healed. "Daughter, your faith has healed you, Go in peace and be freed from your suffering" (Mark 5: 34). The Centurion believed that Jesus could heal his servant by speaking the words. ". . . . I tell you the truth, I have not found anyone in Israel with such great faith "(Matthew 8:10). Talk to others about how God has brought them through. Listen to the testimonies of positive people. Read a good book and pray with a trusted friend. Find that special friend who will help you restore your faith when you are at your weakest point. Read scriptures constantly. "Faith comes from hearing the message, and the message is heard through the word of Christ" (Romans 10:17).

MY FAITH STORY

Teveria was a very special friend when I was at my weakest point. When I was low, she knew just what to say. When I was doing well, she congratulated me for my endurance. Having faith in God that is as small as a mustard seed will see you through Sister Grief. After the deaths of my husband and son, my mother and other family members also talked about faith. Friends and family watched me demonstrate my faith in how I read God's word and attended worship services. When things did not go well, I called upon my faith. I had to believe that things would get better. I continued to worship and fellowship with God. Through everything that has happened in my life, I understand that there was no failure in God. The only failure is in mankind. I knew that God had brought others through and I knew He would do the same for me. In 2008 my family lost a faithful servant and the matriarch of our family. My mother had helped me tremendously over the years. Now, I had to learn to be a woman of strength to help her. Her death added another void in my life. It was only the love of God that helped fill that void. I began to help other elderly women and support them whenever I could. One special mother at my church was a tremendous help to me. Mother Williams reminds me of my dear mother. There is always a storm on the ocean. While I was preparing for my wedding, after ten years of widowhood, my best friend Teveria died suddenly. There it was again, that terrible feeling you feel during Sister Grief. My dear friend was to be a bridesmaid in my wedding; she died ten days before the wedding.

It was the grace of God and my faith that helped me to experience Joy in the midst of the storm. We had a special tribute to my bridesmaid in heaven during the ceremony. I held on to my faith. Faith and friendship are linked in this chapter because to have true faith you must recognize you have a friend who sticks closer than a brother. Yes, Jesus will be your best friend if you let Him. You can call Him during the midnight hour. He's available in the noonday. In fact, His line is never busy; He is always willing to listen.

I encourage you to commune often with your number one friend. God will send other friends long-time and new into your life to share both their faith and friendship. I am constantly amazed at the people I meet who bless my life. I can truly say that people of all races have blessed me with their faith and friendship. I have met friends volunteering at hospice, at church, in classes at St. Mary's Seminary, at work, at the YMCA, in the market or just about anywhere. I have been blessed to meet some wonderful God-fearing people. Thank you God!

HOW CAN FRIENDS SUPPORT YOU?

God in His awesome wisdom will send people here on earth to serve as our good friends to get us through difficult circumstances. If you are a friend, reach out to a grieving sister to offer your love and support. Sister, your responsibility is to accept the friendship. After the death of my nephew in 2011, God sent so many friends into the life of my brother and sister-in-law. Some friends were long-time family friends, other friends were new. There was an outpouring of love from each person's place of employment. Friends are there to support us. They lift us up when we are down. You could share a movie or a good book with a friend. Friends call just when you need a listening ear. God sends different friends to supply different needs. He knows just what each of us needs. Learn to trust friends to be there for you.

MY FRIENDSHIP STORY

I have been blessed over the years with many friends. I have girlfriends who stay in touch with me and support me as I endeavor to support them. There is nothing like a good sister friend. I have friends at work, in my family, at the YMCA, book club friends, sorority friends, and friends from church who encourage and support me in many ways. Some friends like to talk and others like to listen. I have friends from all walks of life. Some friends struggle with more issues than others, but I feel blessed to have them be a part of my life. I have friends who pray with and for me as I pray for them. Now that my daughters are grown, I consider them as friends. The platonic friendship of one close male friend in the first two years after Larry's death and in the first six months after my son Michael's death was invaluable to me. He has proven to truly be a male friend who has no strings attached to the friendship. To this very day, Reggie remains a good friend to me as I hope I am to him. The friendship of males was important to me because I had lost the friendship of my husband and son. Although new friendships cannot replace the special love you have for your loved ones, they can help you cope. One male friend, whom I met in 2002, one year after the death of my son, became my second husband in 2009. We shared a deep friendship that went through various ups and downs, but was able to stand the test of time. Now, my husband is one of my closest friends. Thanks be to God! Sisters, are you sharing with your friends? Everyone should cultivate at least one friendship. Are you allowing a friend to help you to keep the faith? Your faith will get you through the most difficult moments. Yes faith and friendship go hand and hand. Call a friend today. He or she will be glad to hear from you. Sometimes they just don't know what to say. No doubt you have been on his or her mind.

The greatest friend of all is always there to help you. Accept His love. "A man who has friends must himself be friendly. But there is a friend who sticks closer than a brother" (Proverbs 18:24)

FAITH AND FRIENDSHIP—A POEM

Faith and friendship go hand and hand
Without these two it is difficult to stand
Please know that Jesus is the best friend of all
He's a friend who will keep you and never let you fall
Faith will abide in the midst of your pain
Even if for a while the circumstances remain the same
Let your friends help you hold on to your faith
One day this awful pain will end because of your faith
Look to Him who is closer than a brother
He is that special friend like no other
Your grief is conquered and healed in Him!

We All Need Jesus—A POEM

As you reflect on your Sister Grief please remember
        we all need Jesus
I am Mary, His Mother; I was chosen to be His Mother
I watched Him grow

I saw Him crucified, yes I NEED JESUS!
We are Mary and Martha
I Martha, like to have things in order
This house must be straight; the food has to be cooked
Jesus is perfect order; I need Jesus
I'm Mary I love to hear Him speak
I can sit at his feet for days, and I need Jesus
My name Keezy, I have been enslaved
I have been mistreated and brutalized
I NEED JESUS!
My name is Tiffany
I attend Middle School in 2013
I NEED JESUS
My name is Lula Mae
I was born in 1929
I have lived through a lot
I am old, but I have never seen the righteous forsaken
I NEED JESUS!
I am the Woman at the Well
I had many husbands
I was a sinner
He told me all about myself
He gave me Living Water
I NEED JESUS!
I am Darlene
My husband left me with all these children
But the Lord has made a way out of No Way
He has brought me through
Yes, I NEED JESUS!
I am Saphonia
I work in a Fortune 500 Company

I am the assistant to the CEO
My children go to the best schools
But yes, I NEED JESUS!
I am the Woman with an Issue of Blood
No one was able to help me
I touched the hem of His garment
I was healed instantly
I NEED JESUS!
I was just conceived
I have to be in the womb for nine months
I don't even have a name
But I know I will Need Jesus
I am every woman
I am Black, White, Hispanic, Asian or any ethnic group
I encompass all the races
I am on every continent
I have experienced much through the centuries
I knew of His coming before He was born
But once the savior was born, I understood
I NEED JESUS!
We All Need Jesus!

CHAPTER 12

Healed Sisters Living For Jesus

I have chosen this acrostic to share my plan for conquering and surviving Sister Grief.

S - Shock
I - Inspiration
S - Sharing
T - Trust
E - Encouragement
R - Reconciliation
G - Grace
R - Resolution
I - Intimacy
E - Example
F - Faith and Friendship

While the acrostic may seem simplistic, the process is a difficult and personal journey for each of us. It is my desire that this plan for conquering Sister Grief, which was revealed to me by the Holy Spirit, will help a sister while she is in the valley. The valley is not a nice place to be. The Lord God will not leave you in the valley alone. He is there with you, loving you, supporting you and carrying you until you are able to walk again. In life the hard times will come, but it is better to face them with Jesus than all on your own.

To some this final chapter may appear misleading. One may think that healed sisters will never experience pain again. Although I am healed in Jesus, you will see me cry, if we love, and we must, we will experience pain and hurt at some point. I am healed because I have the ability to go on because I understand that Jesus has already won every battle for me. I have faith based on the truth about Jesus to adjust to those valley circumstances, reorganize and move closer to Jesus.

Sisters, He is our anchor. I accept that in this life we will suffer, but that the love of Jesus gives us the strength to move on. None of us can change what happened, but we can decide how we will respond in the valley. My dear sister, I hope this book has been a blessing to you at this difficult time. I pray God heals and comforts you right in the midst of your pain. Lord! Please pour out a blessing my sister won't have room enough to receive. Brothers, I love you too! Peace & Blessings—Yvonne

About the Author

Missionary Yvonne Terry-Lewis is a Christian wife, mother, and grandmother who loves people. Her love for children led to a long and fruitful career in education. Although she retired as an Assistant Principal from Baltimore City Public Schools in 2007, she has never lost her passion for working with children and youth. She has written many songs, poems, short stories, and skits for children during her career. Yvonne has said the tragic loss of her first husband and son transformed her life and has given her a deeper passion for counseling, reading and writing. She earned a Masters from St. MARY'S Seminary in 2009 in Church Ministries-Pastoral Care. **Sister Grief: Defined and Conquered in Jesus** is her first book to be published. Yvonne wants those who are hurting and lost to know that there is Hope in Jesus!